IN MY COMMUNITY / DANS MA COMMUNAUTÉ

PLAYGROUND KINDNESS

LA GENTILLESSE AU TERRAIN DE JEUX

Miranda Kelly

Translation/Traduction :
Claire Savard

A Crabtree Seedlings Book
Collection Crabtree « Les jeunes plantes »

Crabtree Publishing
crabtreebooks.com

Our parents teach us **manners**.

Nos parents nous enseignent les **bonnes manières**.

They teach us to be helpful and kind.

Ils nous enseignent à être utiles et gentils.

Good manners help us get along with others.

Les bonnes manières nous aident à bien s’entendre avec les autres.

Use your manners on the playground.

Utilisons les bonnes manières au terrain de jeux.

Take **turns** and be fair.

Attendons notre **tour** et soyons juste.

You're next!

Suivant!

Do your part to keep the playground clean.

Faisons notre part pour nettoyer le terrain de jeux et le garder propre.

Be sure to **share**.

Assurons-nous de **partager**.

Look out for each other.

Veillons les uns sur les autres.

Be a **good sport**.

Ayons l’**esprit sportif**.

Good game!
Belle partie!

Practice playground kindness every day.

Tous les jours pratiquons la gentillesse au terrain de jeux.

Glossary / Glossaire

good sport (GOOD SPORT): A good sport is someone who uses good manners even when they lose.

esprit sportif (es-pri spor-tif) : Avoir l'esprit sportif, c'est avoir de bonnes manières même quand on perd.

manners (MAN-urz): When you use good manners, you are acting polite and kind.

bonnes manières (bon ma-nyèr) : Quand on utilise les bonnes manières, nous agissons poliment et avec gentillesse.

share (SHAIR): When you share, you are using something with someone else.

partager (par-ta-jé) : Quand tu partages, tu utilises quelque chose avec quelqu'un d'autre.

turns (TURNZ): Turns are chances to do something.

tour (tour) : C'est la chance de faire quelque chose.

Index

School-to-Home Support for Caregivers and Teachers

Crabtree Seedlings books help children grow by letting them practice reading. Here are a few guiding questions to help the reader with building his or her comprehension skills. Possible answers are included.

Before Reading

- What do I think this book is about? I think this book is about being kind to others. It is about how to get along with others on a playground.
- What do I want to learn about this topic? I want to learn about different ways to be kind to others.

During Reading

- I wonder why... I wonder why the children on pages 16 and 17 are sad.
- What have I learned so far? I have learned that some ways to be kind are to share, take turns, and use manners.

After Reading

- What details did I learn about this topic? I learned that good manners teach us how to be helpful and kind. They help us get along with others.
- Read the book again and look for the vocabulary words. I see the word ***turns*** on page 11 and the word ***share*** on page 14. The other vocabulary words are found on pages 22 and 23.

Soutien de l'école à la maison pour les gardien(ne)s et les enseignant(e)s.

Ce livre aide les enfants à se développer grâce à la pratique de la lecture. Voici quelques exemples de questions pour aider le(a) lecteur(-trice) à développer ses capacités de compréhension. Des suggestions de réponses sont indiquées.

Avant la lecture

- Quel est le sujet de ce livre? Je pense que ce livre nous parle d'être gentil(le) avec les autres. C'est de savoir comment se comporter les uns envers les autres au terrain de jeux.
- Qu'est-ce que je veux savoir sur ce sujet? Je veux en savoir plus sur les différentes manières d'être gentil(le) envers les autres.

Durant la lecture

- Je me demande pourquoi... Je me demande pourquoi les enfants, aux pages 16 et 17, sont tristes.
- Qu'est-ce que j'ai appris jusqu'à présent? J'ai appris qu'il y a certaines façons d'être gentil : partager, attendre son tour et avoir de bonnes manières.

Après la lecture

- Nomme quelques détails que tu as retenus. J'ai appris que les bonnes manières nous enseignent à être utile et gentil. Ça nous aide à bien s'entendre avec les autres.
- Écris les mots peu familiers et pose des questions pour mieux comprendre leur signification. Je vois le mot ***tour*** à la page 11 et le mot ***partager*** à la page 14. Les autres mots de vocabulaire se trouvent aux pages 22 et 23.

Crabtree Publishing

crabtreebooks.com 800-387-7650

Print book version produced jointly with Blue Door Education in 2022

Version imprimée du livre produite conjointement avec Blue Door Education en 2021.

Hardcover 978-1-0398-6994-3
Paperback 978-1-0398-6982-0
Ebook (PDF) 978-1-0398-7006-2
Epub 978-1-0398-7018-5

Printed in/Imprimé au Canada

Published in Canada
Publié au Canada
Crabtree Publishing
616 Welland Avenue
St. Catharines, Ontario
L2M 5V6

Published in the United States
Publié aux États-Unis
Crabtree Publishing
347 Fifth Avenue
Suite 1402-145
New York, NY 10016

Photo credits/ Crédits photos: Pages 2-3 © istock.com/ KatarzynaBialasiewicz, page 4 © istock.com /3sbworld, page 5 © istock.com /monkeybusinessimages, pages 6-7 © istock. com/ bowdenimages, page 9 © g istock.com /pointstudio, page 10 © istock.com /monkeybusinessimages, page 12 © istock.com/joebelanger, pages 14-15 © istock.com /Rawpixel, shutterstock.com/antoniodiaz, page 16 © 589088442, page 17 © Ljupco, page 19 © Wavebreakmedia, pages 20-21 © dolgachov
All photos from istockphoto.com except: Cover and page 12-13 © Rawpixel.com, both from Shutterstock.com

Author/Auteure : Miranda Kelly
Translation/Traduction : Claire Savard

Library and Archives Canada
Cataloguing in Publication
Available at the Library and Archives Canada

Library of Congress
Cataloging-in-Publication Data
Available at the Library of Congress